NOUVEAU GRIOT

Dedicated to the griots – past, present and future.

These texts were written with the intention of orality. They have been performed internationally and also exist as audio recordings released between 2004-2016.

NOUVEAU GRIOT

Tanya Evanson

Frontenac House Poetry

Book design: Neil Petrunia, Epix Design
Cover Image: Komi Olaf
Author photo: Temmuz Arsiray

Library and Archives Canada Cataloguing in Publication

Evanson, Tanya, 1972-
[Works. Selections]
Nouveau griot / Tanya Evanson.

Poems.
Issued in print and electronic formats.
ISBN 978-1-927823-84-2 (softcover).--ISBN 978-1-927823-92-7 (PDF)

I. Title.

PS8559.V377N68 2018 C811'.6 C2018-903936-1
C2018-903937-X

Frontenac House gratefully acknowledges the support of the Canada Council for the Arts for our publishing program. We would also like to thank the Government of Alberta Multimedia Development Fund for their support of our publishing program.

Canada Council for the Arts Conseil des Arts du Canada
Alberta Government

Printed and bound in Canada
Published by Frontenac House Ltd.
1648 Bowness Road NW
Calgary, Alberta, T2N 3J9, Canada
Tel: 403-263-7025

frontenachouse.com

Contents

LANGUAGE FOR GODS

ZENSHIP

INVISIBLE WORLD

Bark Lake, BC

It was pre-millennium May, a snowcap bathed in peach
As we left Vancouver for higher ground, all the radio stations went dead
The stillness pushed me into that deep cove of mind, you know the one
With that attitude of a killer spreading love like a touch of madness

Sitting with you in the forest, I lost the wetness in my throat
Couldn't get it back, like an undigested bit of beef
I saw your face pulling into that ego of urban pubescence
Immersed in this new ecosystem of BC's gathered seasons

You can't imagine the rock
You can't imagine the strength

Of a morning pent up in its own vivacity
The earlobe tug of late afternoon wind
The muffled roar of indiscernible animals
The caramel belly of a beachcomber bird

Hands together in prayer, my blood standing on end
You asked me what I like, in a serene stare
As if you haven't known me for the last four years
I say, "The scent of cedar, the swell of waterhip"

Something between us had died
This I knew from the flies hovering above our bed

With all this knowledge, I could not but react with a hard grace
Offering myself obstacles to slice a water so glacial
I foamed at mouth and vein, consolidating all organs
All consciousness of this Birkenhead Lake ache

Nature was my support, my only congratulations
With Her muting of things, Her mumble of rapids, earthquakes, killings
Only She had the permission of touch, to fall in and to feel pain
And how many times can I repeat

How She loves me in half, how She loves me in half
With that jam of a branchwide finger, the tilt of wet attraction

I'll leave you now, burnt red in the metropolitan sun
There is more to know than this needle sharp split
In the Vancouver eloquence
I need the physical world, the ritual arts, inescapable works

And after having had your presence like the howl of all trees
I'll let you go, at the end of the insolent day
I'll let you go, at the end of this pre-millennium May
A snowcap bathed in peach, a snowcap bathed in peach

Al-Mah

This is a tale about a cowgirl, and what a cowgirl she was. The kind you find trying to do her best in a low atmosphere ghost town where sky is star and you can walk into downtown cores, but there are no cars, only rust. She was the kinda ironclad, nubile cowgirl without a driver's license, living about in a characteristically red zone of chakra. Rooted there, monthly, at the very least.

"What a nuisance this low hang," she thought. That waning Moon 'bout a crescent-full, even at noon. Fingernail clipping with a hangover. You look back, Al-Mah is full, hysterical, dreamlike, a good friend of mine. "Why go? When you can stay awhile," he asked, pulling her up to the seaside. His name was … she couldn't quite remember now, but she had been bleeding at the time, that much is true.

He was a teacher off the beaten path in Yelapa, the Mexican Riviera. He instructed young children in great cosmic chemical reactions on the tip of a roadless town, at the edge of a half-moon Bay of Banderas. *Ojala que*, she accepted his invitation.

She was careful. Though traveling in an age of economic enlightenment all she did was spend spend spend her time dodging men offering their seed left, right, centre, at the beach, club, bar, restaurants, streets, cobble-stoned beats – anywhere a cowgirl could possibly meet her cowboy. Who was this cowboy anyway?

"We are birthing a nation of unknowns," she exhaled, releasing infinite atoms into air. This, alongside the continuous passing of babes pressed to full breast. "We are billions of red planets, so similar to Earth! We show evidence of music, dance, seasons, equatorial tilts, polar caps, canyons, crust, core, testimony of a warmer, wetter past, 'cause now we in a cool, dry, Western land, and we are lunatics at best, a vague reflection of even our closest satellite, Al-Mah." That low hang, waning Moon 'bout a crescent-full, even at noon in the blue sky of Puerto Vallarta.

Estoy quemandome. She was burning up when they became lovers through the eyes. It was June, the time of elections. So she resigned her superior post and became that cowgirl. A low pressure, carbon dioxide cowgirl. And the Moon? She just laughed, saying, "You'll never be white like me."

La Costa Peruana

Una piel agrietada de sol
Se presenta en el camino de la costa Peruana

Nos lleva a las dunas de pastel tiznadas
Una eternidad de arena fina

A lo lejos olas sustenidas de agua saltado
Te llenan y te despejan

El desierto y el oceano se juntan
En la costa Peruana

Por las Islas Ballestas, los flamingos en risa de una pierna
Y los foques con heridas de lancha

Dientes felices, lamentos humanos
De macho y de hembra, en la costa Peruana

Movimientos maremotos de piedra y grasa
Un desierto de contaminación pura

Conchas en pilas al lado del camino
Como tumbas reluciendo en el sol central de la costa Peruana

Invisible World

We pulled into the Amazon basin of Las Pampas with that swing of machismo and warm beer, you know the kind of jungle town where heat tells time and a Caribbean flavour pulls into play, to mind. We boarded a dugout canoe and sidestepped onto cyclones, indeed, we are. Blessed as all web-footed birds, Yacuma River was low that day, my friends.

We glided below the aerial roots of trees, panoply and canopy. The water, a pure milk coffee, swallowed us into foam. I placed the lips of my fingers and the piranha snapped from the river's glass ceiling, sharp marine mouths into hand, catfish, minuscule shark. The sky, a woven cloud. Roots, the scalps of slain indigenous, molten into the fiber, broken unlike elastic. *El cielo tejido de nubes. Pasamos por raíces aéreas como cueros cabelludos. Todo suspendido y todo fundido a dentro de la fibra. Roto no como el elástico.*

Threatened by knowledge, we receded into Bolivian night. Directed by his bare feet in the wild, our guide's face hinted at black features. There was also talk of a slur. He was sketched in art, a machete man with protruding jaw, hairless, taut. A guide with sense of direction, a guide with no sense at all, clutching cobras and anacondas both mirrors and enemies. Nude among poisonous trees, he stuck his foot onto fish spines as they lay out to avenge their own gutting.

From the canoe, I threw my skin to bless trains of turtles, high red monkeys, giant white-combed manguari, massive open-mouthed caiman crocs. Capybaras, an unsure species lying somewhere between the guinea pig and the hippopotamus. Clicking sounds abound. At suntanned river bends we swam with freshwater dolphins, extinct to the thought. They rose from underwater hammocks to show us changing skin colour from pale gray to luminescent pink at will. And they're still blamed for unexpected pregnancies in nearby towns.

At camp I ate piranha for irony, drank Bolivian wine for beauty and allowed night frogs on my shoulders to round out the meal. We climbed up to a silvered sunset then down to our canoe in search of croc eyes at night, the red glow of deadly pustules seen easily in dark. We drank water from tree trunks and swung on vines knowing that humans be damned to hack at these forests. Damned by disposition, DNA or demonology.

Back at the village, we slept for long hours in Amazon sun in a courtyard full of mango, avocado and monkey. A bliss so throwing it put the invisible world into view for a fortunate flash. But luck has its limits, and I see that these travels will soon begin to bite at me with the jagged teeth of a bitch who's lost her puppies to the dollar. They will wear me down, question my service, my accountability. What can I say that hasn't already been said? What can I do that hasn't already been done? No matter, I pick at a tick on my right inner thigh, a swing of the locks, and I join in the fruit of life.

Throwing Skin II

No dreams to speak of
As early light threw me out
Like unwanted skin

In places of fields, quadrants of Earth
Split with loose rock walls, broad cacti
Women get off buses in the middle of nowhere

Walking into highland shrub and hidden homes
A sacred lake to the left, cleared as topaz
An occasional garbage dump for bones and batteries

We pass llamas, vicuñas, handless homeless
Weavings and gangs of oversexed dogs
Bolivia, on a cellular level surpasses even the solid meditations

Land here a root blend of corn and quinoa
A diet for starched women, loose bellied from births
Short in stature and strong calved from high altitude work

The breast, central and exposed
Sweating a mother's milk perfume
Porkpie hats off to the side in salutation

Brown forearms slap the child silly
Overturn the land, from barren to big with child
Women, we keepers in culture, in language, in dress

You shout at me with Quechua lungs, "¡*Gringa*!"
I am separate with sepia skin, dull green hills, swollen veins of road
And a rich backpack against the skyline, easy to the touch

We scratch the mother in straight lines
She offers a new vegetable skin
At least hers is never devoid of melanin

Bangkok Business

Hell is business in fine clothing though people are good to me and national-blue orchids grow by the side of expressways, we flourish in the beauty methane. Heat. Motorcycles and surgical masks on all the downtown faces. Tuk tuk taxis. I catch my first elephant in Bangkok traffic.

A cut brings sweet pineapple to glisten the tongue with swollen. Enrage the edge of lip and mouth with desire. Here, the king is god and the god is headless. Heads cut of Buddha statues. Graceful Thai girl hearts turned to stone for the golden king draped in orange robe.

Imagine the reverence, the flavour, the abound. Laundry hangs from all possible hooks, absorbing the thick wind. Patpong girls urge me on. My black-lung highways span the rivers. I buy my own masks and my own cigarettes. My tom yam gung never comes, and when the alternative arrives, it takes my breath and makes it phlegm.

We are near the golden triangle. My fine clothes in decay. Cars know no lanes. Motorcycles, no boundaries. No safety but from air. Advertisements for skin lightening cream send the venom right, while whole classes wait, at five-minute traffic lights.

Ashes

For Ted Joans

Ashes Ashes!
Once the product of combustion
Our energy is now low.
No tar baby broom would even do! To clean up our mess,
Sweep away crying moon fingernails slicing into chest.

Ashes Ashes!
Once the product of devouring
We is now sand through sheet, through warm earth fires.
So I will go south to find me some heat
And maybe even some brown people to eat.

Ashes Ashes!
We are branching out! Through hemispheres
Only, I remember the indigenous geography of lands, oceans, fears.
Of we, we of, dichotomize, sweet grind, smooth pelvic grater.
And my cloven cunt becomes a musky metaphor for our future.

Ashes Ashes!
How do I forget my category?
When it is sometimes I who put me there.
Spanked outta my own rooms with your smooth glow of hand
On the skin of my class.

Ashes Ashes!
My SOS is your breathing. That quick-split emotion.
Right under that swelled curve of neck into blade of yours
The magic of you
The magic of you inside me like a lung.

Ashes Ashes!
Love is energy and does not die
I let it fly
I let it fly
I let it fly

Ashes Ashes!
What happens when we come to the last breath?
When the machine does no good.
How will I grip the event?
When I can't even grip the coming.

Almost Forgot My Bones

A Song for East Van

I was living in a sketched coastal town
Autumn water pouring down like my new motion
It took a while to groove, near this new ocean
But my new motion moves

I found siblings, angelic, pink-haired,
Yellow-glassed, proud-to-be-poor, dare-derelict
They cut me open wide from cunt to pride with sharp love

Pulled out black bones, took me back home
Said, Tanya, love your catacombs
Them is your recesses, your abscesses of mind
So frown down 'cause we all know what racism undermines

Look to yourself,
When you think healing is the hard part
It is effortless effort

Try, because I almost forgot my bones
In this home without no mirrors
Almost forgot my bones
In this home without no mirrors
Of myself, my skin, my kin, my hidden

Just then I thought, who are these new folks
Reminding me that I am black?
Who are these folks? Is this a Vancouver fact?
Or had I forgotten this history

Straight from an 1858 act of black foot
Up from San Fran, stepping onto British Columbian land
Already meant for indigenous holy hand and spirit
We all colonizers, we all colonized

Now when I search for community,
Not only through skin unity do I find love
I find love from above, from below
From four corners of streets
I find movement with beats
We each use to complement each other
And implement change

Got any to spare?
Run it through my hair
If you can get your hand through it

Try, because I almost forgot my bones
In this home without no mirrors
Almost forgot my bones
In this home without no mirrors
Of myself, my skin, my kin, my hidden

I Am at Your Service

Your life is the only book I recommend you read.
It tests you under sun, moon and edifice,
Turn the page with ears open.

This book contains tonics to please all tones,
To solve the crime of hatred, beware the blade of it.
Hatred splits bones that interfere with due process.
Hatred intoxifies water, land, air. It don't care for
Young people, it say. It care only to operate outside
The framework of what is commonly accepted
By we, the common people.

If you ask, "What manner of study is this?"
It is not magic, it is what we call Truth
It becomes one in the turning, no talisman needed.
No need for holy robes tonight, dear. No need
For fascination with a love story other than our own.
No need for weapons to save the microcosmos
We have here. No need for time, no need for space,
No need for people. No need for time, no need for space,
No need for people. And pray we don't get to a time
When there is no space for people, pray, Friend, pray.

But you say, "So and so came, and so and so passed."
How did such brutality come about?
I am only destined to inscribe the emotional pains
Of that inadequacy. Making human history personal to me.
A glorious moment to frost the canopy in whips
Of power and greed. On the sheet of universe
Some see from those nice, affluent balconies.

High rises will not bring us closer to You.
Will not bring us closer to God. The sun goes down
On the ruins we've made of ourselves and we wait.
Arms raised, eyes glazed over.

What cannot be heard has a thunder all its own.
Grown like our common muscle in the chest.
Every pain will be dealt with.
There is Art in hearing this rhythm.
There is Heart in hearing this rhythm.

If only death were this spinning upward, this wave
Lifting into singular pulse, this sudden submission,
This mouth, which closes in this world
And immediately opens with a shout of joy in another.
If only my book didn't take a piece of infinity away from you,
We would all be saved from disservice.
And I am at Your Service, I am at Your Service.

Cooked

In the name of Paris in the springtime
In the name of the tears shed by the prophets of God

What do I do now that I've left my lover for a room with a view? I'm alone in this Paris hotel, drunk and waiting. Dervish, where is your arc of return? Where is the source of my flavour? The source of that, which enriches. I remember the day when you first appeared to me in the tavern. All smooth and working a mean conga. Slim and dangerous. A grazing of your fingers on my right arm and the cooking began. You scooped me up in rituals I hadn't known before. Fed me meals of such divinity – and I'm known for my gluttony. The divorce made me ugly. It increased my waist size. Created arms that did nothing above my head, served only to lift bread and chocolate and liquor to lips. Bread and chocolate and liquor to lips. I tried hard not to be at the mercy of fragments, food or yesterday's mental actions but

In the name of Paris in the springtime
In the name of the tears shed by the prophets of God

What do I do now that I am a solitary traveler, and a poor one at that, hiding under a crust of cautionary sense. A woman in the possible violence of night in new countries. Even old churches here sport gargoyles projected from above to watch over you. But I've got no one to watch my back but my own tattoo. I'm a pilgrim in new landscapes. Travel is a good ritual, like prayer. They are both examples designed to calm the body, focus the heart. Rituals are reminders. Our movement from gross to subtle. *Inshallah*, we find the most beautiful ones but

In the name of Paris in the springtime
In the name of the tears shed by the prophets of God

What do I do now? I will carry myself up from the ocean floor 'cause I got me energy since you closed the door! I will leave the city at full moon. Leave the mistrals, the columns of dog droppings on winding streets, gargoyles at every head thrown back. Gargoyles ain't all that! They are lost lovers jutting from memory with jaws open, ready to get fat. Keep the memory solid. Use as a tool to remove garbage from the Straight Path. Let the gargoyles keep their watch in all their uniqueness and wrath. This magic is real. It comes from my heart, it fills out my hands. It stirs the spoon in the pot, the pencil on the page. It prevents the rot, burns the lead away. This burning is real. There is no end to it, and this burning eventually becomes sweet but

In the name of Paris in the springtime
In the name of the tears shed by the prophets of God

I go round and round in this pot you threw me in, and I thought I could swim. Now you're no longer the chef and I look up to see who's stirring me and it's the hand of God working the spoon of me. I see now, this is the meal of me that I offer as alms. The more I get cooked, the tastier I become. And so I let myself be seized, none of this can be undone. I submit myself to True Love, so that the meal of me can belong to everyone.

Surprise

He lifted me up into breast
He took up the drum in my chest

I am the poet who aims to ease the disease
My own happiness bestowed upon this breeze

Blown from my Love, my Lover, my Beloved
Such a love poured in from all sides

Knowing the onset of my travels
You never misunderstood

The expectation of flight brought a succession of light
From my Love, my Lover, my Beloved

Here we do seasons like the Maya
I add only blood of the kings

I burn your foreskin with love
Offer the resin above

If only to ensure the reigns
You pull me in with Love, my Lover, my Beloved

With my Love, my Lover, my Beloved
With my Love, my Lover, my Beloved

There is no one, surprise, like You

Sauvé

Montre-toi jeune homme déjà vieillard. Montre-moi encore ta liste de génies. Montre-moi encore ton désir niant. Tu bandes quand tu t'écris, et quand tu te relis. Avec mon visage entre tes cuisses et tes mains d'écrivains dans mes cheveux noueux, nous serons libres de toute moquerie, promit, juré.

Buvons le vin affreux d'Azrou, fumons le kif et prenons les encres et les mines en main et le délire naturel par la queue pour vaincre la merveilleuse souffrance. Tâche impossible, tâche inoubliable.

Monte! Je suis une sainte qui fait prière sur ta terrasse! Prenons ensemble le café cassé au Paradis. Mettons le goudron enrobé aux lèvres afin d'inondé le corps matinal avec le brouillard musulman du Maroc.

La douche viendra plus tard et me causera d'innombrables problèmes sociaux. Je me lave aux douches pour hommes car les femmes n'ont que le hammam. Déjà, les oignons brûlés d'hier soir dégagent leurs poisons. J'ai des boutons partout mais tu m'aimes et j'en suis sauvé, peu importe la durée.

Comme les mouches, tu es attiré par mon odeur. Que Dieu soit Louis en observant ces touchés de fou à l'entrée de mes entrailles libérées. Je n'en cache pas ma satisfaction. En effet, je l'annonce.

Aşk

The shell of the Beloved has fallen away
Only the light remains

The body imposes such a suffering. My veins exposed
This heartache is deeper than anyone suspects

You abandoned me. And so like a good disciple
I am abandoning myself as well

It is difficult to move from you
And so I concern myself not with direction

I refuse to sleep, I'm going to protest
By turning night into day

With the movement of one quarter step
If you can take it

Soon my feet will leave the ground
And I may not prevent it from happening

Hands have applauded this Beauty
Drums have been palmed in this Way

I am never awake
But always awakening

I'll think not of how you broke my heart
Only how you mirrored it, brighter than the original

Now that you and I are divorced, I write
My Book of Vows in preparation for the real wedding

I have wept unimaginable tears
Perhaps, this is all my imagination

THE MEMORISTS

I Am Not Together

I want to see with my eyes because I am that vain
I want to sever all my ties because I'm in that much pain
My wanting has not ceased, in fact it has increased
I am coming together, but I am not together

Not a time not a space not a yes not a no
I learnt to pray in these years of listening, but to learn I had to go
Tightrope-walk across Atlantic, horizon bent under my weight
Can I ascend again from this valley? Equilibrium laws say it's not too late

I am coming together, but I am not together

At thirty years of age, I let myself be taught
Not to comprehend understanding is to understand a lot
You said "I" and looked in the mirror, I said "I" and looked at you
I am coming together, but I am not together

My praying has changed, opened into spontaneity
Unsupervised, pre-intellectual quality
It takes only breath to put me here
And make me never ever want to return

I am coming together, but I am not together

The dervish keeps turning for fear of getting lost
The Absolute has no price and we pay it at all cost
Each footstep changes weather, let's hold onto this rope together
I am coming together, but I am not

Slow Man

For Temmuz

May the Marmara Sea turn to wine
So I can be drunk all the time

Look the fish are drunken students
We eat intoxicated schools

Waves cannot lick
These shore stones enough

Slow man, take it slow

Pine fire on the hard beach
Is a small piece of sun we've been given

It indicates our energy
Faces appear when we pay close attention

Slow man, take it slow

Touch me in this way, my Beloved
To increase my silence, my breath

Awaken me in the middle of night
To do what silent Lovers do best

Those moments when planets create sound
Without language or rest

Slow man, take it slow

Salt-rubbed and burnt
A warm Lodos wind from Egyptian south

My body vanishes in your mouth
When you take it slow man, take it slow

Blood and Honey

A humble beginning turns into music
Somewhere during the song, we rejoice at your birth

There is a gift inside you
Do not let it gather dust in a far closet

Unwrap it carefully
With your arms wide open

To open this gift you may need a knife
Try not to cut yourself

But if you do, don't worry
It is a necessary bit of surgery

The gift may have layers and layers of wrapping paper
Pastries of baklava, a hundred blades

Each time you lift a veil
Your fingers may be covered in blood or honey

This work can take years
This work can take a moment

But if you work hard enough to get over this pain or pleasure
The secret inside will be yours

Kan ve Bal

Turkish translation of 'Blood and Honey' by Bejan Matur

Sakin bir başlangıç müziğe dönüşüyor

Bir yerlerinde şarkının
Kutluyoruz doğumunu

Bir hediye var içinde
Toz tutmasına izin verme uzak bir yerde

Aşkla aç
Kolların sonsuz isterken

Bıçağa ihtiyacın olursa
Kesmemeye çalış kendini

Ama kesersen de endişelenme
Cerrahi müdahale gerekli bu hediyede

Kat kat sarmalanmış olabilir
Baklava hamuru, yüz bıçak darbesi

Her örtüyü kaldırışında
Bal yoksa
Kan olacaktır parmaklarında

Yıllar sürebilir bu
Yahut bir an

Bu acı ya da zevkin
Üstesinden gelmek için
Yeterince çalışırsan

Sırrın senin olacaktır

Dervish Weaponry

On our wedding night
I gave you dervish feet full of holes and wide eyes
This, everyone noticed

Alone, I gave you a lower lip
Vanished inside your celibate mouth
In a far corner of Little Istanbul

When we turned to sleep
Breathed *Al Fatiha*
I wiped your face with my prayer

Please, remove this body from the passage
Please, take this tongue from my mouth
This heart contains all the senses one could ever need

Yes, I am heart-supple
But I had never been carved into those positions
At times with breath alone

My whole body became bruised
From our thick red Rifa'i night
El Hamdullillah, let's live in that tavern!

When I left it was early morning through the shades
Your sweat on the pillow, neck wet and pink
Silk brown hair stuck at the temples

A bit of sweet chest exposed
Above the sheet, your edge of hand
Like a sword

Derviş Silahı

Turkish translation of 'Dervish Weaponry' by Bejan Matur

Düğün gecemizde
Sana delinmiş derviş mestimi ve büyük
Gözlerimi verdim
Bunu, herkes farketti

Yalnızken, sana alt dudağımı verdim
Senin bakir ağzında kayboldum
Küçük İstanbul'un ücra bir yerinde

Yatağa döndüğümüzde
Al Fatiha ile nefeslendik
Yüzünü dualarımla yıkadım

Lütfen, bu bedeni, bu dehlizden çıkar
Lütfen, bu dili, bu ağızdan al
Bu kalp ihtiyaç duyacağı tüm
Hislere sahip

Evet ben yumuşak kalpli
Sadece nefesinle getirdiğin hale
Beni kimse getirmedi

O kızıl Rıfai gecede
Tüm gövdem çürüdü
Ama yine de Elhamdüllilah
Yaşayalım o meyhane de

Ben perdelerin gösterdiği o sabahta giderken
Yastıkta terin, ıslak boynun
Alnının tapınağına düşen
Kuzguni siyah saçların

Çarşafların arasından
Gördüğüm göğsün
Ve yarım elin
Sanırım bir kılıç gölgesiydi

Living Is Nothing

I flip the Turkish coffee cup and liquid struggles off the rim and saucer like a fresh cut bleeding in a fine line. I'm not working hard enough and it's making me sick.

I wonder where this is going? Freedom where are you going? Future where have you gone? I am old and round now, who would want me?

I surrender my personality. I surrender my reality. I surrender my knowledge. Nothing I knew before applies here.

I could watch you grow old like this, unveiled. A miracle at the table and in the bed. Living is nothing but rapture.

Tease out the redness in my cheeks. My natural love makeup. Kiss me with an energy from beyond. I become food without form.

We are a possibility of miracles. A flame of intelligent surrender at the heart of solid God. The result of our living must be nothing but rapture. Living is nothing but rapture.

The Importance of Roads

In the invented country
Roads are naughty things

They can exist in the world
But not on the paper of the world

Maps become infidels
And no one believes our unique discoveries

Unmarked roads are the roads we want!
They take us places that, most say, do not exist

One says, Yes, I can get to that place on my donkey
Another says, I've been there and back online

We say, I became the road and disappeared
Not even a map can show you where I went

And peace unto you
If I don't return

Anything less than an angel
And how can we be examples of flight

When light hits the pupil, it shrinks
If only the world could work this way

More light, less world
Less world, more light

Gifted Figs

Fresh figs split easy in the hand
Inside are tiny humans rooted in the skin

Heads bumping up against other heads
It is the overpopulated world turned outside in

If we lived this way, locked inside the skin of Earth
Without the Sun to heal and ripen us

Egos would breathe more air than lungs

Live knowing that sunlight is a gift and not a given
And Light is a given seen only by the gifted few

And you are gifted

The Source

Pine cones are delicious golden sections in conversation with sun. They open arms to worship Shams, their old dry bones symphonic. Pine cone prayer takes its time. If we have patience, we will persevere.

Cows graze on grass sprung from sunlight. We cut Truth open with halal knives because we cannot get enough of this meat. We dress the meat to please the eye. No matter its form, the essence is the same. The light source, what we truly crave.

A couple rowing away into sea can be your future or your past. The boat cuts water into ripple effects. This is a window to the present. See it for what it is. Without looking, without knowing.

A wood white page helps me cut Truth into sheets of understanding. My love is a leaf pressed inside. Speaking can be lamb's wool for the ear. Hell and heaven are not just ideas, they are real.

All of these things are secrets we sometimes know and then not.
All of these things are secrets sometimes known and then forgot.

Human Clay

Let go of belongings
Join friends in the adventure
Don't ask questions

I will take you through a thick vineyard
Where four dogs bark
Do not worry, the dogs are tied to trees

We will climb down hills of fine clay
To soft beach
Where waves lick rock into quartz

Make a well in the sand
For clay and sea water
Hands work like God in the mixing bowl

A thick mud comes
We cover our nude bodies with the stuff
And pass to the other side

Our clay and water selves play games
And disappear with the cliffs
People search for us but find nothing

How can we be silent in this cracking self?
Human clay pinches the skin
To help us remember

Turkish Coffee

Do not try to read your own coffee cup!
It will have no message for you

If Truths do present themselves
Keep them secret

If the sun rises in your cup
Rush to see it next day

That, my friend
Is the real fortune

A bird with feet in its beak can still fly
With an ease you must work on

Don't walk on your hands
Your way is upright, with the other uprights

If there is clarity in your cup
Let your words be equal

Whatever you choose to see
Do not worry, there is no choice

Only arms open wide enough
To be held

By the Truth
In your coffee cup

Istanblues

Here the ferryboats keep time with the call to prayer
Bridges run from Asia to Europe

These are border towns where a river unites land
Neighbours comment only on the world at their disposal

Have we aged beyond thinking?
In the Istanblues

I came to this Miracle City to pray
I asked to burn and fire came

Istanbul flamed my face, my feet, my back
Fevered me for four long years

Aware of flame, aware of light
It blinded me so that I could not even see the world

I prayed for a good man
And now my throat is taking a beating

My language has left me
Like black hair, my voice locks easy

I am at the mercy of strangers
God no longer rides me in the Istanblues

Everything has its place, even in lingual pain
Each moment leads away

The moment itself is the guide
In the Istanblues

Book of Human Being

We are the disappeared
Silent-walkers, truth-observers

With our many veins
To examine

We make inner map readings
Of the good human book

Our pages fill fast
And then slow, they are endless

It is the sort of book
That you can reach with your mind

It will not let the mind
Starve

It is Akashic
Vacuumed contents

An organized madness
Of human experience

And this is the surprise we want
To remember

We are the Memorists, reminders
Of the permanence inside life

Our web, everything
Our centre, Kaabaic nothing

We pray in worship
Of what is really *each other*

We are co-creators and our very creations
Make us one

Notes upon Leaving the Country

Push everything tight into itself and lock the door
Keep tonics in storage for future use
Divorce your business and leave the country with your lover

This new motherhood brings carapaced hands
Use them well on these travels
Do not be at the mercy of fragments, food, or yesterday's mental actions

Move with no concern for direction
But know the quarter turn like the dervish
Value motion, arrive with no expectations

We learn from these things
What the Beloved tried to teach us
By giving our soul to the world

LANGUAGE FOR GODS

Birth Cry

Every mouth that opens sounds different
The music is like a wound, which opens and closes

Instruments loosen hold of each other
And embrace again, inseparable in onslaught
The way I inherited my mother's ability
To cough for years and years and years

Kiss me quick! These are my father's lips
They chew fat with the same relish and excellent overhang
Thick lips hide a sweet tip, but a bitter slave backdrop
Salty joy squared, soursop, Akhenaten is my gumdrop

You are all inside me like a lung
A tongue between slick teeth that age for centuries
Like a dusty piano or a good wine
Teeth are a drawbridge for words that can kill or melt

Poems are assassins! Poems are ice cream!
So like a good, wet, screaming mouth
Around a gun, or a cone, or a microphone,
Soften not the tongue of your state

Don't Not Do It

For John Giornio

Don't walk, run to the Truth
'Cause the Truth is always running away from you, outta sight, outta view and you want to live in that field of vision where wisdom takes formlessness.

Don't walk, run to the Truth
To where flowers whisper forget-me-knots in your fear, which screams and runs outta you so that Truth can turn around and say *Come babe, I catch you*

Don't walk, run to the Truth
Watch your head for low branches by the side of the path. Walk, take a shot, feed it with everything you got, Truth won't die but you–

Don't walk, run to the Truth
Don't keep secrets even from yourself. Messages from mystery can soothe tiny first world traumas.

Don't walk, run to the Truth
Be an echo that blasts through all debris so the world knows something's up. But what? Greed, change, human range? You are the poem struck.

Don't walk, run to the Truth
Your desire drives action. A setting exists. You are the art of the show. You have all the knowledge you need to know.

Don't walk, run to the Truth
Your intricate past fuels the what and why. Crescendos will come, some early, some none, with luck you could come undone, so don't walk, run.

Don't walk, run to the Truth
These verses are united only for a moment. You are a constant instrument of change. A passage of no passage from the now of the gods.

Don't walk, run to the Truth
Freedom includes the body. Freedom includes the mind. You are curiosity leading to curiosity. Thoughts in action all the time.

Don't walk, run to the Truth
It is in the mind, not at the fore but leaking in from behind. Words can kill but not if you get there first. Don't walk, run.

Don't not do it, do it.

Maize-Man Stew

I shall eat you, said the Carib girl
Your tender thigh on rice
I shall cook you in broth, corn, beans and pepper
Unwanted parts can be sold at market
Protein is protein, animal, insects
Heads, arms and legs in earthen jars
Passed among us
Tlacatlaolli, maize-man stew
Forgive me, I eat you.

You found me
On an island in the Aegean Sea
Now that I have you
I offer a feast to friends and family
O my Beloved Sun
You are my mirrored self
Kernels of dry corn sculpted into man
I drink chocolate in your honour
Wear cotton and make a pyramid of my hair
I reclothe in your sacrifice
As new skin that covers Earth each spring
Tlacatlaolli, maize-man stew
Forgive me, I eat you.

Breaking, cutting, sawing marks
Burning patterns, seasoning,
Slippage, bone cakes, human sweetbread
Fresh meat falling from the bone
Virgin marrow full of grease
And fire to cook the brain
Tlacatlaolli, maize-man stew
Forgive me, I eat you.

My God of food and vegetation
O my butterfly
Your thigh to Moctezuma
My sacred sacrifice
I eat God Itself
This is my religion

The African All of It

I polish myself to be bright and blinding
Some can see me, from others I take sight
When I speak in tongues, none work better than silence
I am listening I am listening

The voice can lock but instruments unlock
With the swing of an arm, a pendulum hips
To manipulate breath, control internal chords, takes faith
I am listening I am listening

Whatever your appearance I am listening
Be it air or cuneiform I am listening
We make love I am listening
Everything turns I am listening

This is our mythology

Re: Move

Sitting under a tree
A cherry blossom worm falls on me
I agree, with the worm.

The worm obeys Nature
"Never mind your mind,"
She says.

I cannot disagree
With the worm.
I obey Nature, too.

Who are you? Give me a reason to come to you!
Diviner of birth and vegetation
Marry yourself to yourself

Break your soil for seeds to grow
Break me so I can know
Pure Mind inside Your Nature

My One becomes Two
Who each become one of you
Who are we but variations on a theme

So kiss me!
I am the Wailing Wall, the Black Stone,
I have lips for all your ideas

I ask only that you come.
So when you arrive, I can leave.
Illusion. Rest. I remove myself.

Sitting under a tree
A cherry blossom worm falls on me
I agree, with the worm.

She parts not,
One Truth
From Another

Internetahlagy

Before Records or RAM, radio, radiation
We had slowness. A real root directory. We were tight with the world.

Now, we're in all probability cloud inline, online. Yin Yang binary
Numbers in time. Fractions of our former, warmer selves.

We like. We link. We love. We save. Silently.
Collectively suckling our baby, Internetahlagy.

Our baby has meta-emotions. Baby's got emotions about emotions.
Data about data. Wind about wind.

Baby be metaphysical. Physical without being physical.
Mindful without being mindful, and even more then.

You, me and baby, we move so little but we travel so great.
World moves beyond world at this rate.

Non-stop-this, sidewalk-that, we are walking heads down at clay tablets
Sumerian-style. Extinct papyrus out.

Is this singularity? Are we merging with artificiality?
Machine versus Mind. Nanonaked. Divine.

Will you tap my arm to expose USB porn?
Frontal lobe googlehorn, I'm googling as I speak.

Cloud computing as I eat. Instagramming in my sleep.
All the googalicious googlelatarians feast.

Eat my Facebook! Tweet, swallows, tweet. Tweet tweet.
We like. We link. We love. We save. Silently. Internetahlagy.

We get juice from a box made from oil, sand and farts.
Silicon chip make we blue-lit. A hard drive from the sun.

Finger-tappin. Interwebbin. Radiatin.
Far from fire. O how I miss the time

When palms touched nothing to tell a tale and the light was a fire
Between us. We could really see what we were saying.

We like. We link. We love. We save. Silently.
Internetahlagy. Internetahlagy.

Devil's Bridge

At northeastern tip, pon deh island of Antigua in West Indies, is a remote area known as Indian Town. Wild. Island edge. Atlantic Ocean pon one side, Caribbean Sea pon odah. Crash into each odah. Deep ragin swells. No end. Since time.

At dis place deh is a natural rock bridge. It come straight outta seawater. Erosion. Geological ocean. An ark. A rock. Bridge carved by deh sea from deh saf n deh hard. Limestone ledge. Action breakers. Atlantic waves rollin ovah centuries a wav com faaaaar, from Africa.

How deh water crash up into air n spray we all! As we sit pon deh salt at deh calm n chaotic. What a view! Throw in an egg, it come out like new–ah boiled ah fried. Throw in two, Devil keep one inside. At dis place intellectual slaves committed mass suicide. Slaves from estates min throw themselves in. An Church say deh Devil all tings African …

Jihad waters always rough. Anyone fall over bridge might a nevah com out. Alive. Alive! People, don despair at deh tip of a deep cove of mind. Take deh attitude of divine African ancestry. Spread love gently like a touch of holy madness. Is dis myth? Ah sadness? Legend ah Devil's Bridge be hard, natural evidence.

Antigua, Antigua

Me las an found / Me feel profound
Attachment to Antigua, Antigua

Devil Bridge / Half Moon Bay
Wadadli min please to greet Antigua / from Canada

Yes me wan dat tide / In dem roots me hide
Me heritage an me pride / Antigua, Antigua

But me faddahland emotion be so slim / Me wish me could be pull in
Inside me black skin / Sun inside still strugglin / Antigua, Antigua

Bush tea sugar cane ducanna / New England slave trade patois
Island education inflection / *Seulement* / *Pour moi* / Antigua, Antigua

Salt fish chaddock pawpaw / Hausa tribe from Ghana
Conch palm aloe plantain / AN A RUM TA PUNCH YA HEAD IN

No obeah ye obeah bougainvillea fortune tellah / New life North wife
Take I back to Black life / Antigua, Antigua

Pepperpot an fungi in name only / Jerk chicken goat watah
Locks in a salt watah / Sorrel, bilimbi, lime as a verb / Antigua, Antigua

Far from muddahland tight clothes no sweat / Not like Canada
Cold cold cold cold cold cold FIYAH! / Antigua, Antigua

Me nah Gretzky / Me nah sorry / Me nah tank ye / Me nah foo'
Antigua, Antigua

I an I Caribbean sea / I an I ice pon a tree / I an I me own pickney
I an I me of no me / Antigua, Antigua

And Canada / OOOOOOOOOOOOOOOH Canada / She say
Com back ya! Com back ya! Com back ya

Silent Bang

Why do we make such loud sounds?

Animals don't announce their presence
Silence is the secret to survival for the offline

Smoke signals, talking knots
The Tower Babel to bend the ear of gods

Such a great massage that silence machine
And so much peace to be had

O personal sound shadow
Cover me from all the empty speech

Even the quietest house in the world
Has a silence garden

You could make a noise map of that life
And it would shape shift Pure Essence

Restraint, Ceremony, Tranquility, A Bowl of Tea
Love for you and Love for me

Non clamor sed amor, Make love not noise

Sema (My Heart Is Full of Numbers)

Listen Secret Song Enter Walk Bow Walk Bow

Stand Look Kneel Kiss The Ground Ground Ground Ground

Breathe Kneel Breathe Kneel Strike The Ground Stand Bow

Walk Bow Walk Bow Walk Bow Walk Bow

Walk Bow Walk Bow Walk Stand Stop Strip

Bow Walk Bow Kiss The Hand Bow Walk Look

Turn Stop Bow Rest Turn Stop Bow Rest

Turn Stop Bow Rest Turn Stop Bow Rest

Turn Turn Turn Turn Turn Turn Turn Turn

Turn Turn Turn Turn Turn Turn Turn Turn

Jazz Tonic for Easy Rebirth

There was nothing new in this jazz of my birth
A drunken standard with a twist of lime
These were painful days, my friends
So I went to the doctor this time

My doctor prescribed a tonic
For easy rebirth
Drink pop pop bush, she said
Oat straw and peppermint to ease the girth

Mix these with rainwater and boil for seven days
This will help you keep your cool
'Cause girl, she said, you'll a wear a mask of moisture for the dance
You'll know good and evil for this trance

At night, remove your whiskers and your claws
This will torment genitalia, legs and chest
Administer prayer, libation and sacrifice
So, I did this at my doctor's behest

Once you are reborn into the world, clothe yourself in black
The colour of priestesses and magicians
Wear noisy jewels to perform effectively, she said
But I didn't believe her superstitions

Self-motherhood brings carapaced hands, use them well
Do not be at the mercy of yesterday's actions
Attempt Truth through direct experience
This will help prevent unnecessary reactions

For your renaming, girl, use patterns found in Nature
Cantaloupe Island, Strange Fruit,
Autumn Leaves, Star Dust,
Lilac Wine, Gentle Rain, East of the Sun

There was nothing new in this jazz of my birth
A drunken standard with a twist of lime
These were painful days my friends, still
So I went to the doctor one more time

My doctor prescribed another tonic
For post-partum care
Coconut palm leaf, plum, rum and mother's milk
Drink this love, go on! You'll feel right as rain, light as air

Death for Beginners Part II

Look at me	Regardez-moi
Don't hide your face	Ne cachez pas votre visage
Control yourself	Contrôlez-vous
Do not let others control you	Ne laissez pas les autres vous contrôler
Let this appetite	Laissez cet appétit
Pull you into shapes	Vous tirer en toutes directions
Heart hungry open-heart surgery	Coeur affamé chirurgie à cœur ouvert
Be at this mercy	Cette miséricorde
Freedom is a clever rubbing of hands	Liberté un léger frottement de mains
There is no choice, no separation	Il n'y pas de choix ni de séparation
Take refuge leave refuge	Se réfugier ne pas se réfugier
Wait and see	Attendez et vous verrez
Come back to me	Revenez vers moi
I am your world houri	Je suis votre houri mondiale
Your bliss is my command	Votre joie commandez-la-moi
I was always with you	J'ai toujours été avec vous
Who were you with	Et vous avec qui étiez-vous
I was always with you	J'étais toujours avec vous
Who were you with	Et vous
Wipe your face with this prayer	Essuyer votre visage avec cette prière
And die before you die	Et mourez avant de mourir

ZENSHIP

Qutb

Who here among you is in charge of human souls I desire to meet that one
The one who unlocks the soul from its cage I desire to meet that one
The Lover made whole through sorrow and age I desire
The Threshold Keeper, Middle Way Walker, Axis of Music and Wine
A creature from myth beside us, hidden right here since time
The rigorous drunk and sovereign both, a glance a graze a haze
A possessor of higher knowledge involved with every being in space
No laws in effect, in fact, full flaws in effect, in fact
The moon of every night, in fact, the sun, a secret living in plain sight
In fact, are you here because of me? No. I am here because of your light
Planets reach for immortality, involved with the pull of the sun
Lover Beloveds through space and time a star must be warm for someone
Desire desires desire itself Desire desires itself
Desire desires desire itself Desire desires itself
Desire desires desire itself Desire desires itself
Desire desires desire itself Desire desires itself
When your desire is my desire When my desire yours
When your desire is my desire When my desire yours
When your desire is my desire When my desire yours
Should they crack the door just then the room would be found empty
We are only Mind! We create ideas! The bloodstream from beyond boils in
u s
Breathlessly unveiled Breathlessly unveiled
A hot new temper fills the void the poet's marriage knot
This bridge is my aching back she said my husband a bridge of rock
Until death, the union takes breath
And I am left, I'm left I'm left I'm left

Leg, a Sea

Luba, Chewa, Shona, Hausa
Hutu, Berber, Fula, Zulu
Oromo, Amhara, Sotho, Somali
Igbo, Akan, Afar, Copt
Mande, Mongo, Kanuri, Maghrebi
Yoruba, Tigray-Tigrinya

A sea humility
In each face a crossing
In each mouth honour
Heart, legacy, feet, survival
Mapped hands, black blues
Blood is strong long as it
Jazz-passes on through

A rainbow of veins
Even one-sixteenth recalls its root
A lilt, a nose, a nappiness in hair
A deep gospel voice knows
Sacred is everywhere

This legacy is a home
Not carried outside the body
It is exile of success, raw sun
Your family on the run
Middle Passage 'cross ocean
Iron mask for suicide notion
Apartheid begun
Prison complex of the sun
It is X got the gun he got the gun
And X keep getting the gun

Our family tree is a legacy
Of open arms for armour
You go on or die
But I and I root
Locked hair rising from the tree of life
Lynched, a mob, resisting
Representing anybody
Who's ever been beat down
Which is everybody

We are Egyptology. Afro-Turkey.
Olmeci. Iraqi. Dothraki.
Klingon. C'mon Caribbe-On.
Oceania. Nubia. Negrita. Nigrita.
Ainu. Ati. Tuareg. Aborigine.
Syri. Saudi. Afghani. Kuwaiti.
Bahraini. Kattari. Yemeni. Israeli.
Palestin I. Rast I. Plantation's vagin I.
A house servant givin the stink I.

A Miracle in stone, our bones on throne
A Moor from Spain marooned in Mexico
Zion lions of the seas, idea exchangers early on
Inventing sea legs from vast exploration

Kickin hoppin boppin into global solar plexus
Naming ourselves before enslavement ever had any of us
So let's go back, way back
Lightest to darkest, palest to blackest
Back to no race at all

We were fire sparkers!
Tool crafters! Goddess worshippers all!
Burying the dead, clothed in animals
Sewn from needles made of bone

We were storytellers! Cave painters!
Nature-observing ritualizers!
Bartering the big bang of human consciousness
Until acceleration of civilizations
Created genetic differences

Hominidae, homininae, hominini, hominina
We all walked Ethiopia
Hominidae, homininae, hominini, hominina
Black legs into infinity
Hominidae, homininae, hominini, hominina
One common mama, so far, so root

This medicine is human psychology
Anti-apocalyptology
A working towards collective memory
History, the giant forgetting of legacy
The Mysteries, original ingenuity
Artistry of the tribe called humanity
All we. From mama. All we. From Africa.
All we a legacy of stars.

Coming and going from same source
A sea of faces one face
A dark spacious wave
All the way home, all the way home

That legacy's me in me
That legacy's me in you
One mother memory
Leg, a Sea

Temple Exercises

Physiology flutter. Atrial fibrillation. Brother.
Repetition rhythms. Extra beats we all have it.
I seen my father's heart green on a black ultrasound screen.
He been up to Montreal from his girlfriend Caribbean.
Crossed the Quebec Hospital Sistine system and still sick of it.
Dad's knee tried to get itself together in the thick of it.
Stiff knee swollen broke but it was the Heart
That needed attention.
As oldest child in the family
I was given dervish duties in the temple
And training began in the kitchen.
Meditating on knees for days.
Food was brought and requests were made to relieve the bowels.
Clean it, cook it, move it, doctor, pray, wash, sweep. Repeat.
Clean it, cook it, move it, doctor, pray, wash, sweep. Repeat.
Physiology flutter. Atrial fibrillation. Brother.
Repetition rhythms. Extra beats we all have it.
That day my father lay on his left side, shirtless. Elbow to hand
Hold head up, hospital bed. Ultrasound machine running jelly clean
Across his black nativity chest. Nonchalantly breathing.
Silenced by it all.
But never missing a beat.
Dad the doctor became a very patient patient patient patient patient.
Then cardiologist brother, he jump at green screen and say,
Look at that heart valve!
It open and close like a Mercedes Benz sign.
I say, *No. It's a vagina, Yo.* He say, *Oh!*
There are extra beats though.
What? Extra beats though.
What? It's ok.
Every heart has extra heart beats.
Four chambers in the heart making chamber music hit hop.
Two atria pump in, two ventricle out. Simultaneous.
Left side separate from right.
The two never communicate but to turn vascular music to Life.
Flight. Wind. A Wave. Nothing constricts at once.
The heart contracts and relaxes
Like a dark fist getting things done

Even from stem cells in a petri dish
Heart cells beat on and on and on
Physiology flutter. Atrial fibrillation. Brother.
Repetition rhythms. Extra beats. We all have it.
My heart is the Mud Mosque at Djenné
Beating for the Universe itself. Every year the rains take it
And faith alone rebuilds it. My heart is the pyramids of Kush.
And the entire complex of Giza.
My heart is the very Uluru. The original Dome of the Rock.
Mecca at Hajj is just us dancing around our own soft Black Stone.
The Wailing Wall says lean in and kiss me
Lhasa is a mountain gym
The Ganges say get naked and swim
Stonehenge looks up at the sky
As I fly to you on Island.
With your heart medicine in a box. Father.
Physiology flutter. Atrial fibrillation. Brother.
Repetition rhythms. Extra beats. We all have it.
Out of all my temples on earth, visit my grave at Giza
And ask for Ma'at, the Mother of Truth.
She will weigh your heart against a feather, Father.
Physiology flutter. Atrial fibrillation. Brother.
Repetition rhythms. Extra beats. We all have it.
A repeat retreat   To the most sacred point   In the most sacred point
In the most sacred point   In the most sacred point
In the most sacred point   In the most sacred point   The Heart
The Heart   The Heart   The Heart

Apocalypsiata

Send Out Protective Animals
Because some will come
In fancy cars or ragged dress
Seeking blackmail

Prepare Your Weapons Well
Brute response is based
On brute preservation
In the name of survival keep trust alive

Power To The Peaceful
There's a gun remove the bullets
You can always eat money
It's just wood or metal, alchemize

Stay Close To Home
Keep a lover nearby
So you will have meat
When the power goes out

Say No To Injury
When the body works we don't feel it
One small cut is cause for complaint
But slow death in Apocalypsiata

Soon There Will Be Nothing
Left to burn
Books, beds
Bodies on the barbie

We Are All On Fire
But too busy online
To do anything about it
Like Like Like Like throw away the key

As Our Time Together
Draws to a close
My eyes spill an ocean
That could drown the world

Apocalypse Is Subjective
The Maya were right
It's not the end of the world
It just floods like it in Apocalypsiata

Knowledge Blues

Knowledge is a thought on something
Take it off. Take it all off.
Take your knowledge off piece by piece
Peace Peace Peace Peace Peace

You. Talking Lover. Undress.
Turn to quiet nakedness.
Beyond the Body, beyond the Book.
Remove your shirt. Skirt.
Lower pants to reveal a happy line
Of fine non-alphabetizing
Leading to the mound of Truth.

No need for opinions.
No categories or judgments.
No inside. No outside. All unveiled.

Whether our thoughts are there or not.
It is It is It is

Take it off. Take it all off.
Take your knowledge off piece by piece
Peace Peace Peace Peace Peace

Remove accessories, undergarments
Hair pieces too
Until there's nothing left to say.
No theories to interrupt the way.

Now that you're naked, skin comes next
But it hold on tight to itself.
Forethought and foreskin alike.
Higher intuition is your birthright
No assembly required.

Whether our thoughts are there or not.
It is It is It is

Take it off. Take it all off.
Take your knowledge off piece by piece
Peace Peace Peace Peace Peace

Remove limits from sources
Deduct all taxes
Keep yourself at zero or one.
Now that you have so little artifice
Observe muscles, organs, bones and blood.
Let the knowledge muscle atrophy
And all the rest lets go.
Without skin blood is ocean
Without lung is there air
Let go let go let go

Launch this business of thoughtlessness
You'll see it shall succeed.
No identity no you no me
No I no I no I Take it off. All off.
Take your knowledge off piece by piece
Peace Peace Peace Peace
P e a c e p e a s p e a f a s f d s o j c c j f f i s a k l d l n d f i j g j d l k j s d o v m w e i
skfdkdfjhjfjdhfdoooedwa!dweebah!deedladeebahbabahxjvljxlkcjxkjccnladeeda
xckaxcjskguislmsalcxkxclvbjfofsussaidjsdaboobadaboobadaboobadadaddadada
djfdommhbfijhvfsvjklnvofjvhsfuihfdjdskvfojxnfoijvfiiofhgibdsjfhmcfjdvcjghfd
fhnfgevndissjxsdkemgfjvdicdjshufhgfuvdcdusfvfdhbfuvhdvundughdfjdifduofhi
hfdijghfduhfdihdfivsdklfsokvncjxvfvhftrdigheodjfkgherogheqrfmdgiodfajiapjie
kritopfyhobndfjbnvkkibfdmvj Hey a hey a hey a hey a hey aya hay ya hay ya
hay ya hay ya hay ya hay ya hay ya hay ya hay ya hay ya hay ya hay ya hay ya
hay ya hay ya hay ya hay ya hay ya hay ya hay ya hay ya hay ya hay ya hay ya
hay ya hay ya hay ya hay ya hay ya hay ya hay ya hay hay hay hay hay hay hay
hay hay hay hay hay hay hay hay hay hay hay hay hay hay hay hay hay hay
hay hay hay hay hay hay hay hay hay hay hay hay hay hay hay hay hay hay
hay hay hay hay hay hay hay hay hay hay hay hay hay hay hay hay Huuuuuuu
uuuuuuuuuuuuuuuuuuuuuuuuuuuuuuuuuuuuuuuuuuuuuuuuuuuuuuuuu

Act of Creation

Original Persian by Najm al-Din Razi, 13th century

Listen to know
Know to do
Do to progress
Progress to arrive
Arrive to find
Find to lose
Lose your self

Lose your self
To be found
Let your self be found
By your self
Find your self again
To know your self
Know your self to love
And love to be loved

Then everything
Will become clear

Empty Empties

Doctors collect waste from the body
They cut it open at the front back sideways
And scoop out hard fat spheres

They send us to pathology to determine our exact toxicity
But how can anything in existence be inessential
When opposites are all so true

Garbage collectors collect waste from the street
They have excellent abdominals from crunching into piles of rock
Push it from one place to another because nobody want this gold

At the city treasure chest we see the Pyramid Mount, this is our own
Future but we don't want it. No matter how much our garbage grows
The meek shall scratch at that crust in what we think are faraway lands

Any downtown can be a disposable plastic latte
A feminist sometime crash at her very desk from so much white hot milk
Upon waking she push her empty cup into a bigger cup

Every night a browner woman empties the empties into a larger trophy
But she never feel like a winner because her circumstance is the very
Definition of blues. Lucky there be television for bearability

But then I saw five fat TVs working the sidewalk just the other day
No one wants 'em big anymore. Operational but thick is out of fashion
We put it out the curb and expect someones to take it–oops–

His boot kicked in the screen, no one seen him treat her like trash
Anyway he got a new flat top machine, and she work good for awhile
But turn four year old and die too soon (computer crash course 101)

We renew but there are fewer ways to enter her body now
That vagina machina sewn shut and all we gots
A stack-a-laptops women with all the necessary holes but no juice

We put atoms together that can never get loose
We fear the empty cell the essence of our living
I could go on and on about garbage but in Nature there's no such thing

Mundo Gumbo

In gumbo, you begin with the one ingredient that requires the most attention. Your Life. Get born! For a soul you need flour and fat in equal proportion.

Slowly whip the flour into fat in small amounts until a roux is born brown. If it burns even slightly throw it out and start all over again.

A woman is born with all the eggs she will ever need. Seed come and go. If you find some seed you like, you make gumbo.

Roux is to gumbo as blues is to jazz. Like your ego fry the okra in a separate pan. Fry yourself until dry then set yourself aside. Sit quietly. Let anything unnecessary seep out of you completely.

Next, to the vessel, add the holy trinity. Woman man and spiritus mundi. Or bell pepper onion and celery. Let us not forget holy quadrality and add two-spirit, intersex, queer, transgender Scotch bonnet pepper to the Mundo Gumbo reality.

Our aroma thickens as we age. Garlic, bay leaf, cayenne pepper.
Fish, chicken or sausage if the day is right. This is the midway mark of your life. You been cooking for 30 years at least.

Put the okra back in because Saturn be Returning to the place she was at when you were born. This is called a cosmic bitch slap. It's gonna hit you in the pot. Take your breath away tear you apart! Mixing spoon moving violently this way and that. Tomatoes flying at you left, right, centre. Chicken water drowning you until you sink or swim. But if you remember that you were born from balance, then this is when your flavour really begins.

Simmer for another 20 years or so. Get cooked good. Let your own life reduce down. You are slow soul food, friend, and things are so much faster now.

Freedom seasoning. Improvise your ending. May it be balanced to the taste. You need bitter, sour, spicy, salty, umami, sweet so that you'll serve well with rice, snow, sand, or city concrete beneath your feet. The essence of you what we'll eat.

Finishing salt is holy sassafras. Petals of parsley in your wake. People the world over will gather to feast on the result of your life plus heat. People of all nationalities. With a whole lotta integratin' going on.

The aroma of your life is at stake. Your ability to fuse all of life's ingredients until your flavours awake. One or two guests may still have to pass the hot sauce between them but we will all raise a glass as we spoon out your honour. Your dish is dangerous. Its strength will come from balance and burn. A bit of soul food from a friend, my friend. Not from me, this, from Mundo Gumbo we learn.

Rock Blanket

I've enjoyed hanging out on Earth. It's been fun, really.
The minor genocides, drone wars, chronic ice ages, uncivilizations
And such. It's been great, really. Great.

On earth as in space there's pressure between bones, blood feuds
Between us. Gravity or not we gain weight, go vertigo. All the dark organs
Splatter. The whole planet red molasses on a church wall.

In brief bursts Earth is tough.
You got dust, dirt, salt, water, flame and quartz all right at the surface
Organics above and below but rich middle ground forgot.

Separation again and again. A spine extends. Surprise, nigger!
Your darkest humans are at the crust of things, scabs wounded
Over and over. Such solid attractive skin, that random melanin,

A great absorber of much needed light. Resilient regolith.
The rock blanket that covers all. The largest organ of the body.
A balanced black bargain, if you let it. Holds everything in the balance.

Your skin of earth can go from absent to hundreds of meters in thickness
From instantaneously born to hundreds of millions of years old.
From root up to nothing but the thin film between us we are ferocity

Still skin lightening, skin tightening
Picking and scratching at the dark cutaneous layer of everything.
Chemical peels of the nuclear persuasion.

Pursed lips the smoke of industry. Toxic ocean botulism bombs.
Your wrinkles have become the deep Himalayas, Atlas, Andes, Alps
There is no blood flow there.

So I say again, it's been fun, really. I've had a ball on this ball
But zero gravity calls. I would invite, but not everyone can be
A multiplanet species. And you are indeed expensive beings.

Take care the primary for now. Never mind my lofty plans.
Tend to your gardens. Stay here.
Do not go up there and cosmetically reengineer galactic atmospheres.

Do not warm the moon or the red dust dot of Mars.
Do not make her nice and warm. She cold. Of another lot.
She will not nurture you like this Gaia here.

Evolve yes. Just not too far out the Milky Way, ya hear?
Tend to your gardens. The soil of living, your own rich middle ground.
The planet membrane itself. Rock blanket. Hold it down. Lock it down.

Thank you, and good luck.

"Empty Empties" and "Rock Blanket" appeared in *Arc Poetry Magazine* (2016). "Cooked" appeared in *Where The Nights Are Twice As Long* (Goose Lane 2015). "Apocalypsiata" appeared in *Womanspeak* (2014). "Antigua, Antigua" and "The African All of It" appeared in *The Great Black North* (Frontenac House 2013). "Bangkok Business" appeared in *Bluesprint-Black British Columbian Literature And Orature* (Arsenal Pulp Press 2002).

Tanya Evanson is an Antiguan-Canadian writer, performer, producer and educator from Tiohtià:ke/Montreal. She presents spoken word internationally, has released four audio recordings, and is director of the Banff Centre Spoken Word Program and ANU live art. Notable performances include Suoni per il Popolo, Vancouver Writers Festival, Ottawa International Writers' Festival, Ubud Writers Festival, Tasmanian Poetry Festival, Edinburgh Book Festival and Glastonbury Festival. Her first book of poetry *Bothism* (2017 Ekstasis Editions) is performed as a live videopoem and other recent publications include *Arc Poetry Magazine, WSQ* Feminist Press, *Making Room-40 Years of Room Magazine* (Caitlin Press), and *Resist Much/Obey Little* (Dispatches Editions). She is a past recipient of the Sheri-D Wilson Golden Beret Award and was Poet of Honour at the 2013 Canadian Festival of Spoken Word. She moonlights as a whirling dervish.

mothertonguemedia.com